NATURAL SCIENCE
PRIMARY 3

BY ME

ACTIVITY BOOK

Unit 1	The human body	2
Unit 2	Look after yourself	8
Unit 3	Living things	14
Unit 4	Mammals and birds	20
Unit 5	Reptiles, amphibians and fish	26
Unit 6	Invertebrates	32
Unit 7	Matter, materials and mixtures	38
Unit 8	Energy	44
Unit 9	Machines	50
	Glossary	56

UNIT 1 The human body

1 Write the parts of the body. Draw lines.

1. *ear*
2. ______
3. ______
4. ______
5. ______
6. ______
7. ______
8. ______
9. ______
10. ______

2 Read the definitions and write the joints.

a. It connects the foot to the lower leg. *ankle*

b. It connects the lower arm to the upper arm. ______

c. These connect our arms to our torso. ______

d. This connects our legs to our torso. ______

3 Cross out the mistake in each sentence. Write the correct word or words.

a. The circulatory system moves ~~food~~ through the heart and around the body. *blood*

b. Blood gives our body nutrients and carbon dioxide. ____________

c. The heart is divided into two parts. ____________

4 Order the sentences to describe how the respiratory system works.

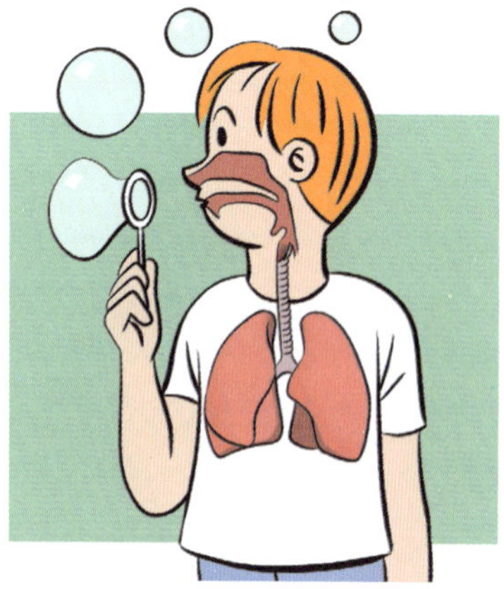

a. Air goes down into our lungs. ☐

b. We breath in air through our nose and mouth. ☐

c. Oxygen is passed to the circulatory system, where it moves around our body. ☐

5 Complete the text about the digestive system.

The digestive system is a group of organs that work together to help us digest *food*.

We take in food through our ____________. It passes down into our stomach and ____________.

The intestine separates the nutrients from the ____________ and expels the waste from our body.

The nutrients are passed to the ____________ system, where they move around the body.

6 Write the words under the pictures.

~~heart~~	lungs	intestine	stomach

a

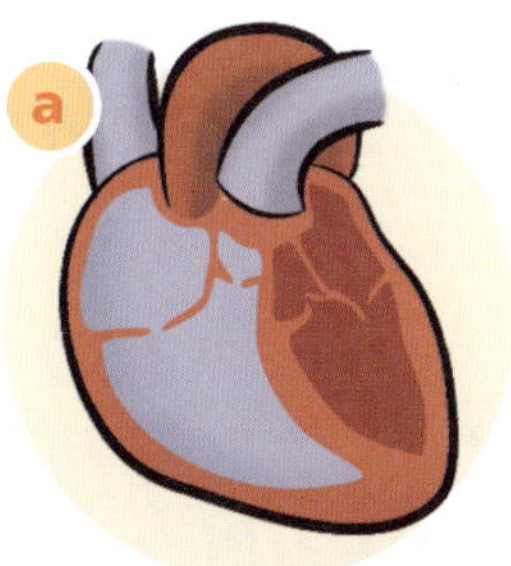

heart

b

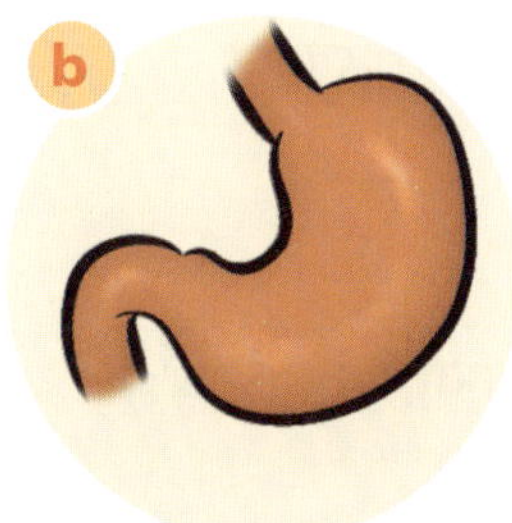

____

c

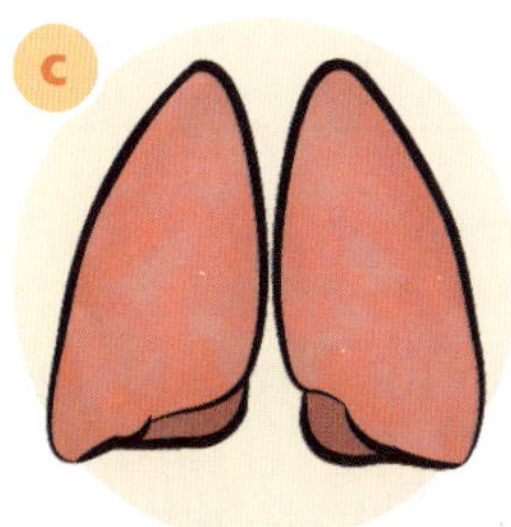

____

d

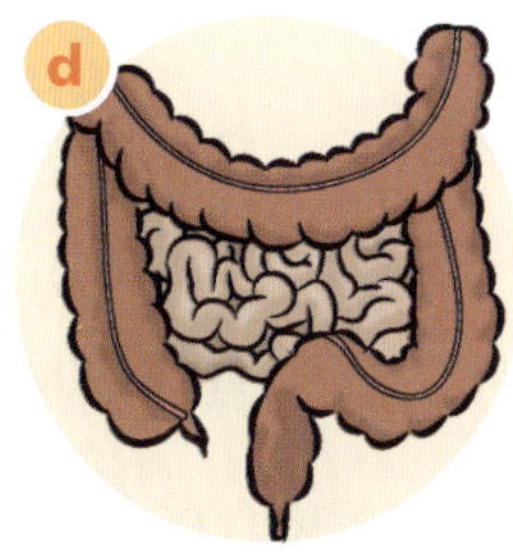

____

7 Look at the photos. Write sentences.

a

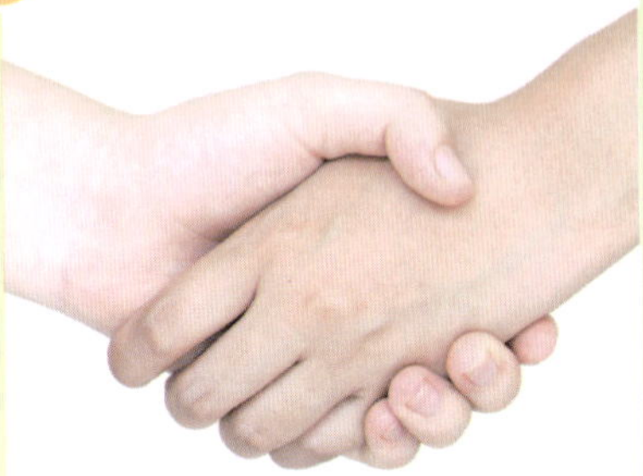

Our skin is the organ we use to touch.

b

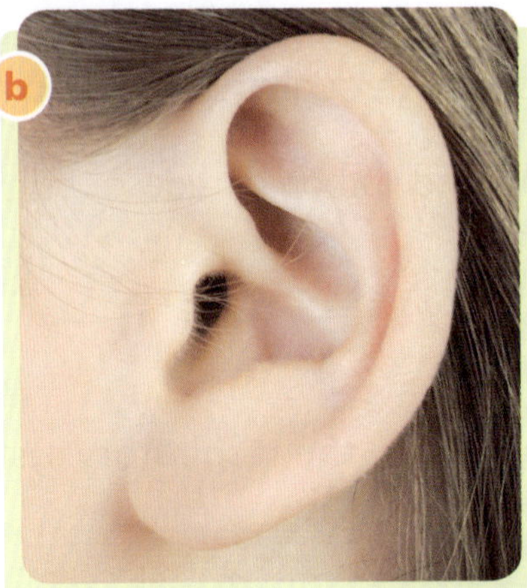

____

c

____

d

____

e

____

8 Complete the sentences using the words in the box.

brain	~~pupil~~	protect	retina

a. Light enters the eye through the *pupil*.

b. The light goes through the lens and makes an image on the ________.

c. The retina sends information to the ________.

d. Eyebrows, eyelashes and eyelids ________ our eyes.

9 Order the sentences to explain how we hear.

a. The brain reads the signals and tells us what we can hear. ☐

b. Sound waves enter through the outer ear. ☐

c. The waves hit the eardrum in the middle ear and make it vibrate. ☐

d. The liquid in the inner ear moves and sends signals to the brain. ☐

10 How do these things taste? Write sentences.

a

b

c

d

Olives taste bitter. ______ ______ ______

______ ______ ______ ______

11 How do these things feel? Use the words from the box. You can use more than one word.

hot	cold	smooth	hard	rough	soft

a

b

c

______ ______ ______

______ ______ ______

Find out at home!

1 Investigate different tastes at home:

1. Choose five items of food. Ask your mum or dad to choose five different items of food.
2. Do a taste test:
   - Close your eyes.
   - Ask your mum or dad to pass you their food items.
   - Taste them. How do they taste?
   - Open your eyes. What were they?
   - Ask your mum or dad to close their eyes and repeat the test with your food items.
3. Write your results in the table.

	Me		My mum / dad	
	Food	Taste	Food	Taste
1				
2				
3				
4				
5				

a. How many food items did you guess correctly?

b. Which foods and tastes did you like? Which didn't you like?

Skills check

1 Read the text. Choose the right words and write them on the lines.

Look after your eyes

There are lots of things you can do to look after your eyes:

1. ___*Turn*___ the lights on when it is getting dark.
2. Wear sunglasses and a ______ on sunny days.
3. Never look directly at the ______.
4. Tell your teacher if you cannot see the board or the text in your ______ clearly.
5. If you wear glasses, don't let other ______ use them. Don't wear other people's glasses.

1. Place	Turn	Have
2. hat	scarf	coat
3. board	book	Sun
4. book	pencil case	lunch
5. animals	person	people

UNIT 2 Look after yourself

1 Which section in the supermarket do the food items below belong in? Complete the table.

bread

potatoes

chicken

yoghurt

lettuce

sausages

cheese

salmon

muffin

tuna

Bakery	Fruit and vegetables	Fish	Meat	Dairy
		salmon		

2 Circle the healthy foods blue and the unhealthy foods red. Complete the tables.

Healthy foods

Unhealthy foods
cola

3 Complete the sentences using the words in the box.

nervous system	calcium	vegetables	vitamins	fat	eggs
protein	dairy	carbohydrates	~~cereals~~		

a Pasta, rice and *cereals* contain fibre and ______________.

b Fruit and ______________ are full of ______________ and minerals.

c Milk and ______________ products contain ______________.

d ______________ and iron help us build muscle and make us strong. Meat, fish and ______________ contain protein.

e Foods rich in ______________ help our brain and ______________ ______________.

4 Write sentences about the food in the photos.

a 

Fish contains protein. Protein helps us...

____

b 

____

____

c 

____

____

5 Look at the healthy habits. Write sentences about yourself.

a

- In my free time I like to *relax. I also like to* ______________________________ .

b

- I brush my teeth after ______________________________ .

c

- I do some exercise every ______________________________ .

6 Look at the photos. Write the health problems. There are more words than you need.

tiredness	a cold	a stomach upset	tooth decay	obesity

a

____

b

____

c

____

7 Order the stages of life from the youngest to the oldest.

adolescent ~~baby~~ adult elderly child

baby ______ ______ ______ ______ ______

8 Match the stages of life to how we change and grow up.

a. When we're babies,	our bodies continue to grow and change.
b. When we're children,	we eat, sleep and discover the world around us.
c. When we're adolescents,	we can walk, talk and play.
d. When we're adults,	we sometimes need people to look after us.
e. When we're elderly,	our bodies stop growing.

9 Complete the text about growing up.

We all look *different* and change as we get older. When we're babies, we need our ______ to do everything for us. We grow into ______ and we learn many things. When we're ______, our bodies continue to grow and change. When we're adults, our bodies stop ______.

Finally, when we are ______, we have a lot of experience, but sometimes we need people to do things for us.

Find out at home!

1 Investigate food labels at home:

1. Read the information about food labels below.
2. Read the labels on five different food products in your home.
3. Answer the questions below.

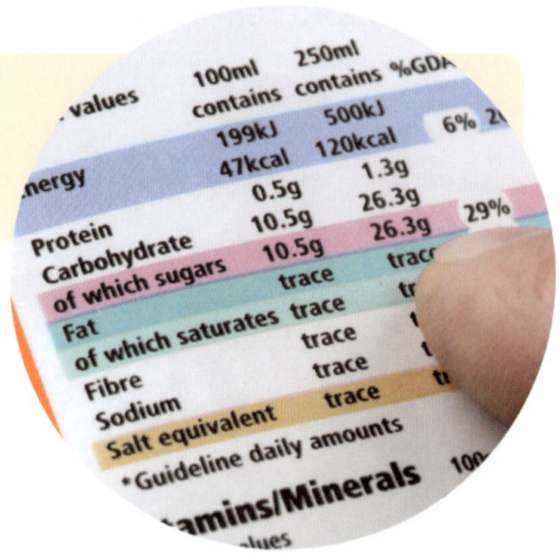

Food labels

Food labels help us choose between healthy and unhealthy products. These labels contain information about:

Energy: This is measured in kilojoules (kj) or calories (cal). When we eat and drink, we put energy into our bodies.

Fat: Foods that contain more than 17.5% fat are unhealthy and make us put on weight.

Carbohydrates and fibre: These give us lots of energy and help our digestion.

Sugar: Foods that contain more than 22.5% sugar are unhealthy. They can make you fat and they are also bad for your teeth.

Protein: This helps us to build muscle and make us strong.

Salt and sodium: Foods that contain more than 1.5% salt or 0.6% sodium are unhealthy and bad for your heart.

Which food product in your home contains ...

a. the most energy? ____________________

b. the most fat? ____________________

c. the most sugar? ____________________

d. the most salt and sodium? ____________________

Do any of your food products contain too much fat, sugar, salt or sodium?

____

____

Skills check

1 Look and read. Write some words to complete the sentences below. You can use one, two or three words.

Be a good sport

A *good sport* is a person who doesn't get angry when they lose.

It is important to learn how to lose and not get annoyed. Everybody likes winning but we can't always win, so remember to control your feelings. It's ok to feel disappointed when you lose, but don't make the winners feel bad by getting angry or upset.

If someone doesn't follow the rules of a game, stay calm. Try to talk about it and find a solution. Remember that it's just a game, so have fun and be a good sport!

a. A person who doesn't get angry when they lose is called *a good sport*.

b. It is important to control ________________ when you lose a game.

c. Sometimes people don't ________________ the rules of the game.

d. If someone doesn't play the game properly, try to talk about it and find a ________________.

UNIT 3 Living things

1 Circle the living things green and the non-living things black.

2 Complete the table with the living and non-living things from the picture.

Living things	Non-living things	
	natural	man-made
dog		

3 Complete the concept maps.

4 Complete the sentences with the words from the concept maps.

a. Some *organisms*, like bacteria, can only be seen under a microscope.

b. ____________ feed on other living things that are decomposing.

c. People make ____________ things.

d. Most ____________ can move from one place to another.

e. Water is an example of a ____________ non-living thing.

f. ____________ are born from seeds or spores.

5 Complete the sentences about life processes and match the texts to the photos.

plants communicating ~~food~~ living things interact

a. **Nutrition:** All living things need *food* for energy and to grow. People and animals eat ________________ or other animals. Plants use sunlight to make their own food.

b. **Interaction:** All living things ________________. Moving, touching and ________________ are some forms of interaction.

c. **Reproduction:** All living things reproduce. Reproduction means making new ________________.

6 Match and write true sentences about interaction.

People	make	sounds and use movement.
Plants	move	towards the Sun.
Animals	talk	to each other.

a. *People talk to each other.*

b. ________________

c. ________________

7 Complete the texts using the words in the box. Match the texts to the photos.

grasses	bushes	~~trees~~	flexible	trunk	taller	longer	branches

a. *Trees* have a thick, woody stem called a ______. The ______ grow high above the ground.

b. ______ have a soft stem. They are thin, ______ and usually short.

c. ______ have low branches. They are ______ than grasses and live ______.

8 Read about hibernation and answer the questions.

Some animals hibernate during winter because it is extremely cold and food is difficult to find. Bears, frogs and bats are some of the animals that hibernate to adapt to their environment. During hibernation, animals go into a deep sleep to use less energy. Their heart beats more slowly and their body temperature lowers. Animals that hibernate eat extra food during autumn to prepare for the winter months. This extra food becomes extra body fat, which is used as energy while sleeping.

a. Why do some animals hibernate in winter?

Animals hibernate in winter because it is cold and difficult to find food.

b. How do animals prepare for hibernation?

______

c. How does an animal's body temperature and heartbeat change during hibernation?

______

Find out at home!

1 Investigate living and non-living things:

1. Find a photo which contains at least two living things and two non-living things.
2. Stick the photo in the space below.
3. Answer the questions.

Which living and non-living things can you see in the photo?

How are the living things interacting?

Skills check

1 Look and read. Choose the correct words and write them on the lines.

Protect the environment

Living things are all around us. They live in (1) *water*, land and air. We can help living things by protecting the environment.

We can help the environment by saving water. Turn off the (2) ______________ when you are brushing your (3) ______________. You can also take a shower instead of a bath.

Creating less waste is also important. You can (4) ______________ and reuse plastic, glass and paper products.

Ride your bike or (5) ______________ to school. Lots of cars on the (6) ______________ create lots of pollution.

Make a plan to protect the environment and start today.

road

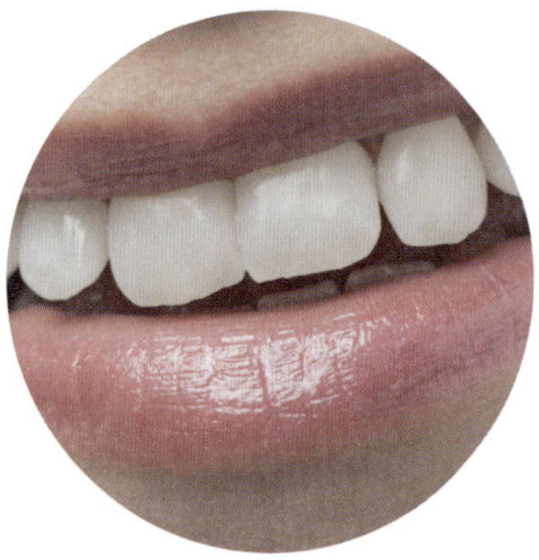
teeth

walk

recycle

water

tap

UNIT 4 Mammals and birds

1. Complete the sentences.

vertebrates or **invertebrates**

a. ______________ have a backbone.

b. ______________ don't have a backbone.

mammals or **birds**

a. ______________ have feathers.

b. ______________ have fur or hair.

viviparous or **oviparous**

a. Some animals are ______________. They lay eggs.

b. Some animals are ______________. They have live babies.

herbivores, carnivores or **omnivores**

a. Animals that eat other animals are called ______________.

b. Animals that eat only plants are called ______________.

c. ______________ eat animals and plants.

2. Complete the table with information about the farm animals.

	Name of animal	Type of animal	Reproduction	Nutrition
	*cow*	*mammal*	*viviparous*	*herbivore*

3 Complete the crossword.

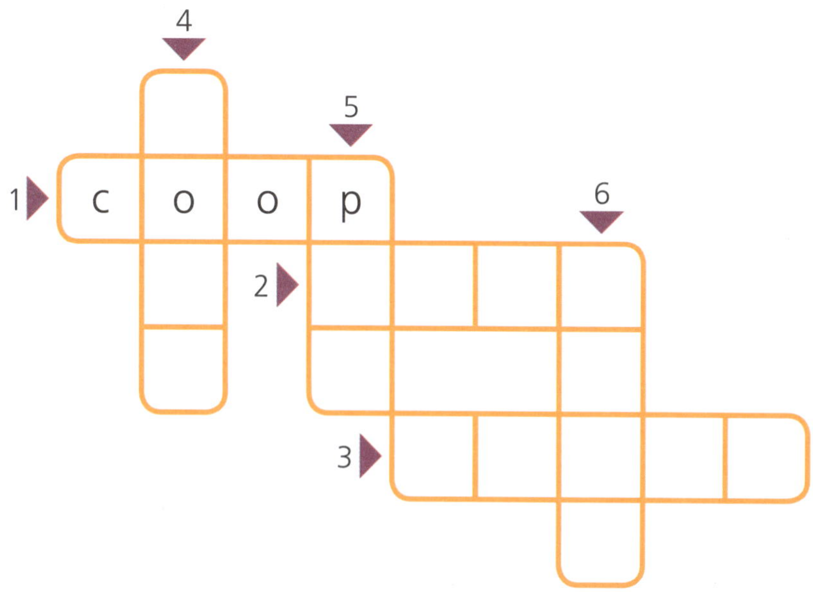

Clues across:

1. Chickens live in a …
2. Chickens lay many …
3. Sheep live in a …

Clues down:

4. We use sheep's fur to make …
5. Pigs live in a …
6. Cows live in a field or a …

4 Write sentences about these baby farm animals.

a

A baby chicken is called a chick.

b

c

d

5 Complete the table with information about the different mammals.

Mammals	Where it lives *land or water*	How it moves *number of legs or flippers*	What it eats *herbivore, carnivore or omnivore*
dog			
giraffe			
bear			
gorilla			
dolphin			

6 How are these two mammals the same? How are they different? Complete the text.

Both elephants and whales are very big mammals. They're both *viviparous* and they both breathe with their ______________. Elephants have four ______________, but whales have ______________. Elephants live on ______________ but whales live in ______________. Elephants are ______________ whereas whales can be carnivores or omnivores.

7 Use the information above to complete the Venn diagram.

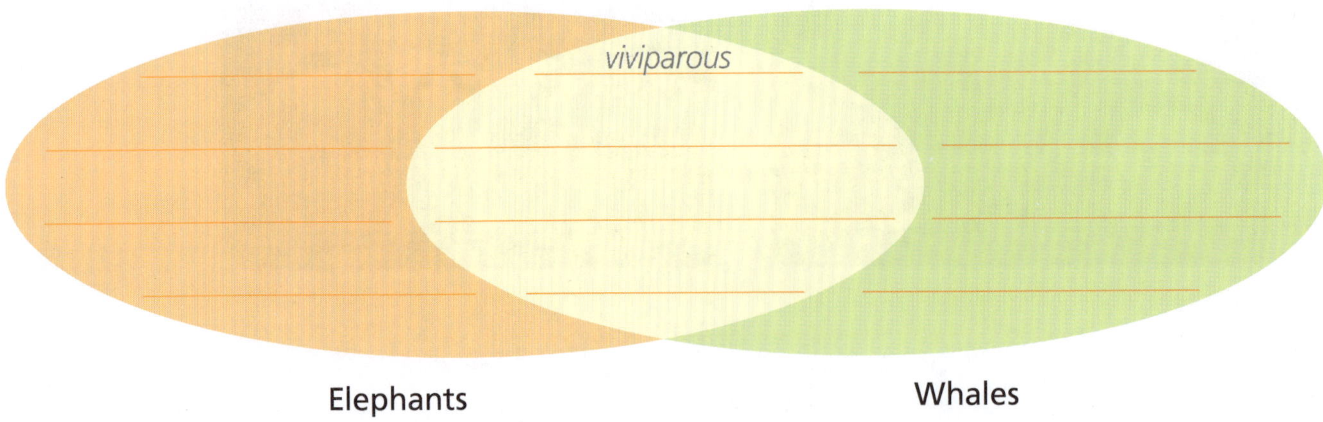

8 **Complete the text about birds.**

Birds are *vertebrates*, which means that they have a backbone. Birds breathe in oxygen from the air with their __________. They're __________, which means that they lay eggs. All birds have a __________ which they use for eating. All birds have __________, but not all birds can fly.

9 **Look at the photos. Read and answer the questions.**

seagull

hawk

sunbird

sparrow

a. Which bird eats meat? __________

b. Which bird eats nuts and seeds? __________

c. Which bird catches and eats fish? __________

d. Which bird drinks nectar from flowers? __________

10 **Write the sentences in the correct boxes. Some sentences go in both boxes.**

They move using wings. They have feathers. They lay eggs. They have fur or hair. They breathe with their lungs. They have a backbone. They have four legs.

They move using wings.

Find out at home!

1 Investigate a bird:

1. Choose a bird and find information about it.
2. Stick a photo or draw a picture of the bird in the space below.
3. Complete the table.

Name of bird	
Physical characteristics	
Type of beak	
Which area of the world does it live in?	
Nutrition	
Can it fly?	
Interesting fact	

Skills check

1 Look and read. Write some words to complete the sentences below. You can use one, two or three words.

Taking care of your pet

Having a pet is fun but it is also a big responsibility. Pets are living things and they need people to take care of them.

Pets need food and clean water. It is important to know what kind of food to give your pet and how often you should feed them.

Pets also need shelter. Shelter is a place where pets can live safely. Shelter can be a cage, a tank or a doghouse.

Exercise helps your pet to be happy and healthy. Take time every day to play with your pet.

Remember that just like you, your pet needs lots of love and attention!

a. Pets need people to *take care of* them.

b. It is important to know how often you should ______________ your pet.

c. Shelter is a place where pets can ______________ .

d. You should play with your pet ______________ .

UNIT 5 Reptiles, amphibians and fish

1 Classify the different vertebrates.

shark

snake

frog

monkey

carp

parrot

giraffe

crocodile

sparrow

salamander

Vertebrates				
Mammals	Birds	Fish	Reptiles	Amphibians
		shark		

2 Complete the sentences with *reptiles*, *amphibians* or *fish*.

a. *Fish* can be carnivores, herbivores or omnivores. They breathe through their gills.

b. Baby ______________ breathe through their gills. Adults breathe with their lungs and through their skin.

c. ______________ have moist skin.

d. ______________ have scales that protect their body. Most have four limbs.

3 Read the questions about reptiles and tick (✓) the correct answers.

1 How do reptiles breathe?

- **a.** Through their gills. ☐
- **b.** With their lungs. ✓
- **c.** Through their moist skin. ☐

2 Where do reptiles live?

- **a.** They live in all types of habitats. ☐
- **b.** They only live in hot climates. ☐
- **c.** They live in all types of habitats, except in very cold climates. ☐

3 How do reptiles reproduce?

- **a.** All reptiles are oviparous. ☐
- **b.** Most baby reptiles are born live. ☐
- **c.** Most reptiles are oviparous. ☐

4 How can we classify reptiles?

- **a.** They're all herbivores. ☐
- **b.** They're all carnivores. ☐
- **c.** Most are carnivores. ☐

4 Complete the descriptions of the reptiles.

oviparous | carnivores | omnivores | lungs | four limbs | ~~scales~~ | slither | swim

Cobras have a long body that is covered with *scales*. They are very good hunters and can __________ very quickly. Cobras are __________ and eat other snakes, birds and small mammals.

Alligators usually live in freshwater. They have four limbs but they can __________ faster than they can walk. They breathe with their __________. Alligators are __________ and lay their eggs on land which is near water.

Tortoises live on land. They have __________ and a hard shell. They can hide inside their shell for protection. Most tortoises are herbivores but some are __________ and eat both plants and meat.

5 **Read about salamanders and answer the questions.**

Salamanders look like lizards, but they are different. Lizards have scales but salamanders have damp skin. Baby salamanders live in water and breathe with their gills. Then they grow and change through a process called metamorphosis. Adult salamanders live on land and in water. They breathe with their lungs and through their skin.

a. How are salamanders and lizards different? *Lizards have scales but salamanders have damp skin.*

b. Where do baby salamanders live? ____________________

c. Where do adult salamanders live? ____________________

d. How do adult salamanders breathe? ____________________

6 **Look at the photos and complete the life cycle of a frog with the words in the box.**

front	tail	tadpoles	~~eggs~~	back

They lose their __________ and leave the water.

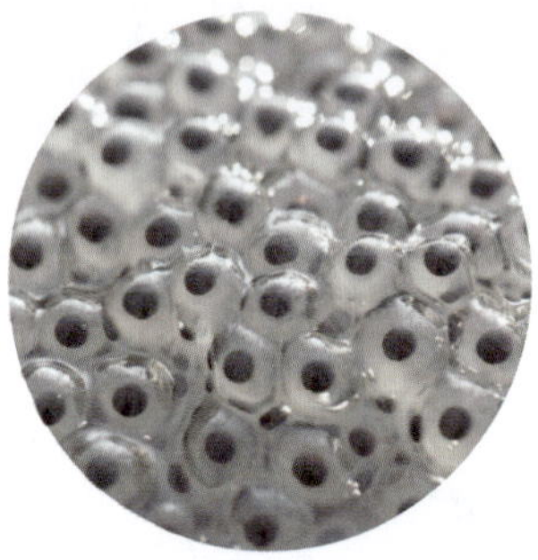

An adult frog lays *eggs*.

__________ hatch from the eggs.

They develop __________ legs.

They develop __________ legs.

7 Label the parts of the fish.

8 Write the sentences in the Venn diagram.

Their fins help them to move.	~~They are viviparous.~~	They breathe with their gills.
They are omnivores.	They are oviparous.	They are carnivores.

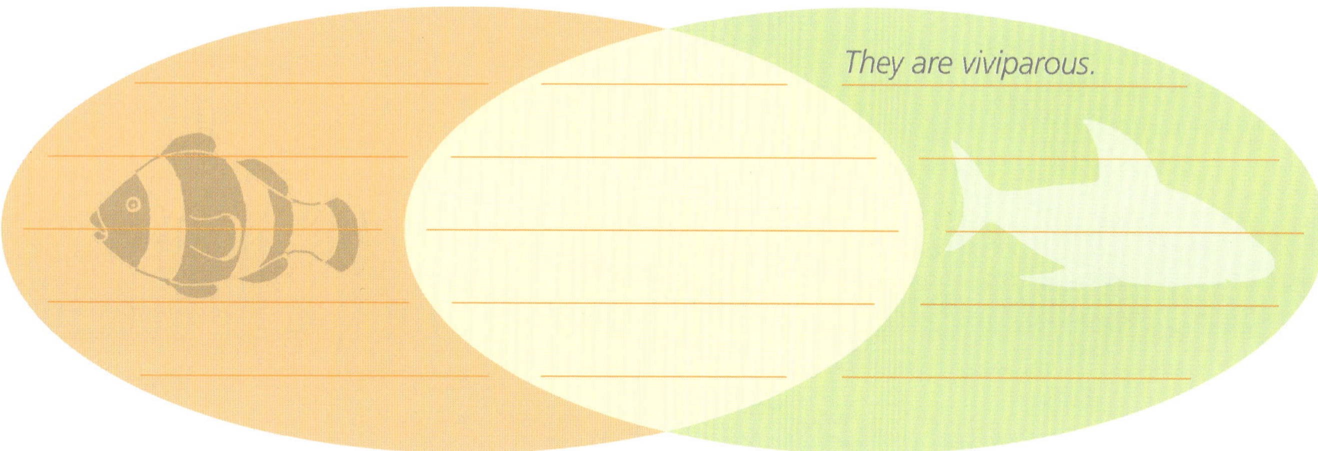

clown fish   sharks

9 Write the correct animal covering on the line.

Which animal covering is for...

a. flying and keeping birds warm? ______________________

b. keeping mammals warm on land? ______________________

c. protecting reptiles and fish? ______________________

fur or hair
feathers
scales

Find out at home!

1 Investigate a reptile, amphibian or fish:

1. Find information about a reptile, amphibian or fish.
2. Stick a photo or draw a picture of the animal in the space below.
3. Complete the concept map.

Name of animal

Vertebrate group

Physical characteristics

Reproduction

Nutrition

Respiration

An interesting fact

Skills check

1 Read the text and choose the best answer.

1. Tom: Hi, Mary. Is this a frog?
   Mary: **a.** Yes, I think it.
   b. Yes, that's it.
   c. Yes, it is.

2. Tom: Can I pick it up?
   Mary: **a.** No. You shouldn't do.
   b. No. You shall take it out of the water.
   c. No. You shouldn't take it out of the water.

3. Tom: You shouldn't touch wild animals or move them from their homes, should you?
   Mary: **a.** No, you shouldn't.
   b. No, don't do it.
   c No, you shouldn't that.

4. Tom: Ok, but can I feed it?
   Mary: **a.** Feeding wild animals can making them sick.
   b. Feeding wild animals can make them sick.
   c. To feed wild animals makes them sick.

5. Tom: Then what can we do?
   Mary: **a.** We can enjoy them at their natural habitat.
   b. We can enjoy them in their natural habitat.
   c. We could enjoy them to their natural habitat.

UNIT 6 Invertebrates

1 Complete the sentences about invertebrates.

a. Invertebrates are the ____________________ group of animals on Earth.

b. Invertebrates all have one thing in common; they don't have a ____________________.

c. Many invertebrates have an ____________________ or a shell to protect their body.

2 Complete the table with information about the invertebrates.

Invertebrates	**Where it lives** *land or water*	**How it moves** *walk, crawl or fly*	**Protection** *shell, exoskeleton or soft body*	**Number of legs**
 ladybird	*land*	*walk, fly*	*shell*	*six*
 crab				
 earthworm				
 tarantula				
 snail				

③ Classify the arthropods.

moth

black widow

centipede

mantis

shrimp

tarantula

lobster

millipede

Arthropods			
Insects	**Arachnids**	**Myriapods**	**Crustaceans**
moth			

④ Write *insects, arachnids, myriapods or crustaceans* on the lines below.

a. *Crustaceans* have a thick exoskeleton.

b. ______________ have lots of legs.

c. Most ______________ have wings.

d. Most ______________ have eight eyes.

e. ______________ and ______________ have two antennae.

f. Most ______________ have eight legs and two claws.

5 Complete the descriptions of the molluscs.

gastropods bivalves ~~cephalopods~~ shells soft body antennae land oxygen tentacles

squid

Cephalopods live in water. They have a ____________ and a large head. The also have ____________. They can change colour to hide from predators.

oyster

All ____________ have two ____________ and live in water. They open their shell to pull water in for ____________ and food.

sea slug

____________ are the largest group of molluscs. They have a soft body and live on ____________ and in water. Some have a hard protective shell. Their eyes are at the end of their ____________.

6 Classify these other invertebrates.

jellyfish

fireworm

starfish

sea anemone

sea urchin

Annelids Long, segmented body	**Cnidarians** Shaped like a bell or tubes	**Echinoderms** Body parts radiate from a central point.
	jellyfish	

7 Label the insect's body using the words in the box.

antennae	~~thorax~~	head	abdomen	wings

a. *thorax*

b. ______

c. ______

d. ______

e. ______

8 Complete the life cycle of a butterfly using the words in the box.

Adult butterflies lay ______.

The eggs hatch. The babies, called ______, grow to become caterpillars.

A caterpillar attaches itself to a leaf and transforms into a ______.

A ______ emerges from the chrysalis.

Find out at home!

1 Investigate arthropods:

1. Walk around your neighbourhood or visit a local park, field or beach.
2. Find two different arthropods and observe them carefully.
3. Compare their similiarities and differences and complete the Venn diagram below.

Arthropod 1

Arthropod 2

Skills check

1. Look and read. Write some words to complete the sentences below. You can use one, two or three words.

Little helpers

When you hear the buzzing sound of a fly or find ants in your home, you might think that invertebrates are annoying.

But many invertebrates are helpful and very important for the environment. Worms live in the soil and help bring oxygen, water and nutrients to the roots of plants. Many insects, like bees, help plants to reproduce. They carry pollen between flowers. The flowers use the pollen to produce seeds.

Some invertebrates, like spiders, eat other invertebrates that can be dangerous, like mosquitoes. People eat some invertebrates too, like prawns or squid.

a. Although some invertebrates can be annoying, many of them are *helpful*.

b. Worms bring oxygen, water and nutrients ________________ of plants.

c. Many insects help plants to ________________.

d. Some invertebrates ________________ that can be dangerous.

UNIT 7 Matter, materials and mixtures

1 Complete the sentences with *matter* or *materials*.

a. Everything on our planet is made up of ____________________.

b. We use different ____________________ like wood, plastic and metal to make things.

2 Look at the photos and complete the sentences using the words in the box. Some words can be used more than once.

Materials	Properties
glass fabric metal plastic	flexible rigid absorbent waterproof

a

b

c

d

a. This is made of *metal*. It's *rigid* and *waterproof*.

b. This is made of ____________. It's ____________ and ____________.

c. This is made of ____________. It's ____________ and ____________.

d. This is made of ____________. It's ____________ and ____________.

3 Match and make sentences about the properties of materials.

a. A fragile material	is difficult to break.
b. A flexible material	breaks easily.
c. A rigid material	can change shape easily.
d. A resistant material	doesn't change shape easily.

4 Complete the sentences with *physical change* or *chemical change*.

a. When matter changes shape, size or state it is called a *physical change*.

b. When matter changes into different matter it is called a ______________________.

c. Combustion is an example of a ______________________.

d. Freezing water to make ice is an example of a ______________________.

5 Look at the photos. Are these physical or chemical changes in matter? Write sentences.

a

This is a physical change because the matter changes shape.

b

____

c

____

d

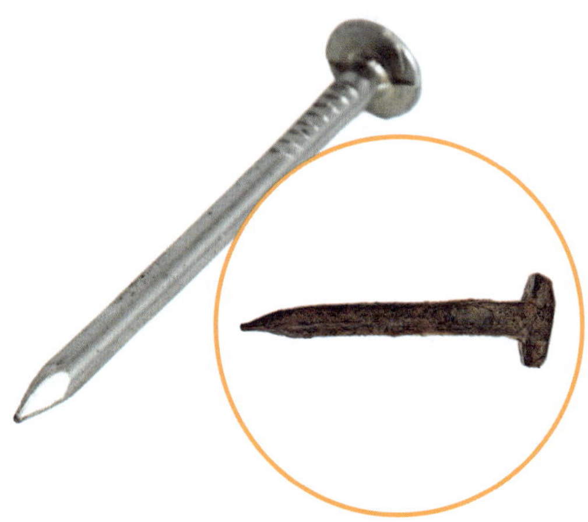

____

6 Look at the photos. How many different materials can you see in each mixture?

a

cereal

b

salt water

c

fruit salad

d

chocolate milkshake

a. *I can see three materials in this mixture.*

b. ______

c. ______

d. ______

7 Match and write true sentences about separating mixtures.

Sieving	is good for	separating a solid that is dissolved in a liquid.
Filtering		separating solids of different sizes.
Evaporating		separating solids and liquids.

a. ______

b. ______

c. ______

8 Which mixtures in activity 6 do you think you can separate? How can you separate them?

You can use filtering to separate...

______

______

______

9 Complete the sentences with *natural material* or *manufactured material*.

a. A *natural material* comes from living things or from the ground.

b. A ______________________ is processed from natural materials or chemicals.

c. Wood is an example of a ______________________.

d. Paper is an example of a ______________________.

10 Classify the materials.

~~cotton~~ glass wool crude oil plastic fabric feathers paper

Natural materials		Manufactured materials	
cotton			

11 How is paper manufactured? Order the sentences and write.

☐

After that, the pulp is dried and made flat.

☐

Finally, the paper is made into sheets.

☐

Next, it is mixed with special products and made into pulp.

1

First, the wood is cut into small pieces.

1. *First, the wood is cut into small pieces.*
2. ______________________
3. ______________________
4. ______________________

Find out at home!

1 Investigate materials in your home:

1. Take photos or draw pictures of three objects in your home.
2. Observe the materials and the properties of each object.
3. Write a text about each object. Include the information below:
   - The name of the object.
   - What materials it is made of.
   - Are the materials natural or manufactured?
   - Its properties.
   - What the object is used for.

Skills check

1 Look and read. Write *yes* or *no*. There are two examples.

1. The table is made of wood. *yes*
2. Wood is fragile. *no*
3. There are four plastic cups in the picture. ______
4. Plastic is a natural material. ______
5. The girl is twisting her serviette. ______
6. There is a chemical reaction called combustion happening. ______
7. There is a mixture in a bowl on the table. ______
8. The little boy is evaporating the rocks from the sand. ______
9. They can recycle the plastic cups and the plastic bottle. ______
10. All the objects in this picture are made up of matter. ______

UNIT 8 Energy

1 Circle the correct type of energy.

a

sound energy

kinetic energy

light energy

b

electrical energy

chemical energy

kinetic energy

c

light energy

electrical energy

kinetic energy

d

electrical energy

thermal energy

kinetic energy

e

light energy

sound energy

electrical energy

f

thermal energy

light energy

chemical energy

2 Match and write true sentences about energy.

Energy can

Energy can't

- be created.
- be changed from one type to another.
- be destroyed.
- be found everywhere around us.

a. *Energy can be changed from one type to another.*

b. ______________________________

c. ______________________________

d. ______________________________

③ Read the clues and complete the crossword.

ACROSS

2. ____________ energy travels from hotter objects to cooler objects.

5. The faster an object moves, the more ____________ energy it has.

6. We can use water, wind or the sun to produce ____________ energy.

DOWN

1. Food contains ____________ energy which our body turns into kinetic or thermal energy.

3. ____________ energy can travel 300,000 km per second.

4. When we talk we produce ____________ energy.

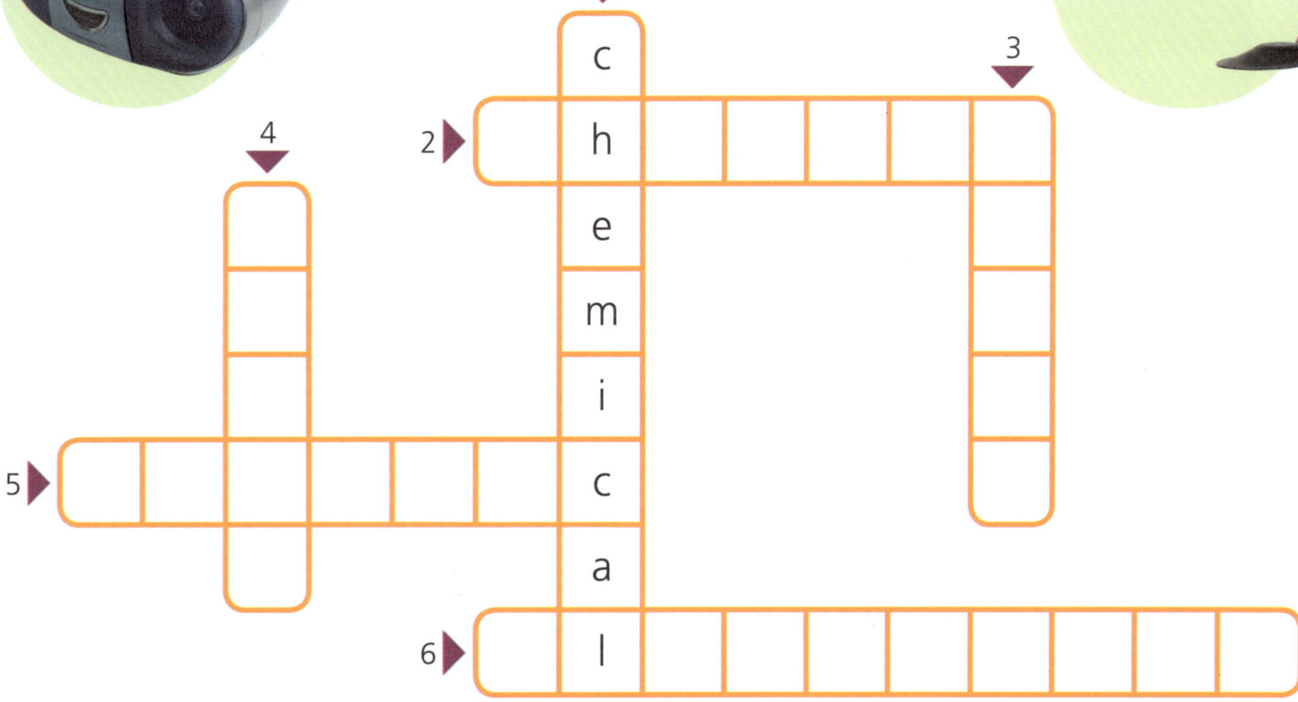

4 Complete the concept map.

Energy sources

- non-renewable
  - ______
  - oil
  - ______
- ______
  - ______
  - ______
  - water

5 Complete the sentences about renewable energy sources using the words in the boxes.

water	wind	sun

wind turbines	~~Solar panels~~	hydroelectric

a. *Solar panels* transform energy from the ______ into electrical and thermal energy.

b. ______ transform ______ energy into electrical energy.

c. ______ power stations transform energy from the movement of ______ into electrical energy.

6 Read about pollution and answer the questions.

Non-renewable energy sources cause pollution and harm the environment. The three major types of pollution are air, water and land pollution. Burning fossil fuels is the biggest cause of air pollution. We can use renewable energy from the Sun, wind and water to help the environment. Renewable energy souces do not cause pollution and they do not run out, unlike non-renewable sources.

a. What are the three major types of pollution?

____

b. What is the number one cause of air pollution?

____

c. What can we do to reduce the amount of pollution and help the environment?

____

7 Use the information about renewable and non-renewable resources to complete the Venn diagram.

~~can be replaced~~ source of energy come from nature cause pollution fossil fuels
used to produce electricity don't cause pollution can't be replaced

Non-renewable resources Renewable resources

Find out at home!

1. Investigate different ways you can save energy at home:

1. Read the information about saving energy.
2. Look around your home and think about different ways you and your family can save energy.
3. Complete the table below.

In our homes we use a lot of electricity. We use it to provide our homes with light, heating, hot water and air conditioning. We also use electricity to power electrical appliances like TVs, fridges and washing machines. But there are ways we can use less electricity and save energy. For example, we can turn off the light when we leave a room or have a shower instead of a bath.

Area which we can save energy in:	How we can save energy:
Heating/Cooling	
Water	
Lighting	
Electrical Appliances	
Other	

Skills check

1 Read about staying cool and saving energy in the summer.
Choose the correct words and write them on the lines.

Example

Open this to let a cool breeze in the house. *a window*

Hints

a. You can read a book instead of watching this. ____________

b. This machine keeps you cool and uses less energy than an air conditioner. ____________

c. You can eat this for lunch instead of cooking. ____________

d. Plant one of these for extra shade on hot days. ____________

e. You can wear these instead of shoes to stay cool. ____________

f. This is a place where you can go swimming. ____________

a fan

a window

a television

a sandwich

a tree

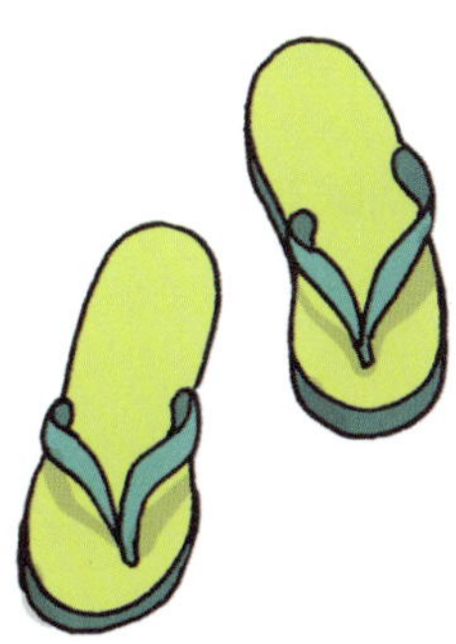

sandals

the beach

a bike

UNIT 9 Machines

1 Match and make true sentences about machines.

A machine •	• is made up of simple machines.
A simple machine •	• is something we use to make work easier.
A complex machine •	• has few or no moving parts.

2 Label the simple machines.

wedge   pulley   wheel and axle   screw   ~~inclined plane~~   lever

a

inclined plane

b

____

c

____

d

____

e
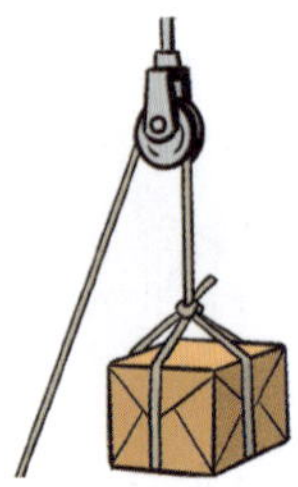

____

f
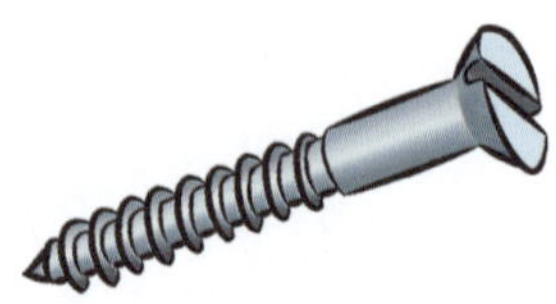

____

3 Complete the sentences using the names of the simple machines.

a. We use a ______________ to move objects from one place to another.

b. We use an ______________ to move objects up and down different levels.

c. We use a ______________ to cut objects.

d. We use a ______________ to lift and lower heavy objects.

e. We use a ______________ to hold things together or lift objects.

f. We use a ______________ to lift objects.

④ Identify the simple machines.

a

wheel and axle

b

c

d
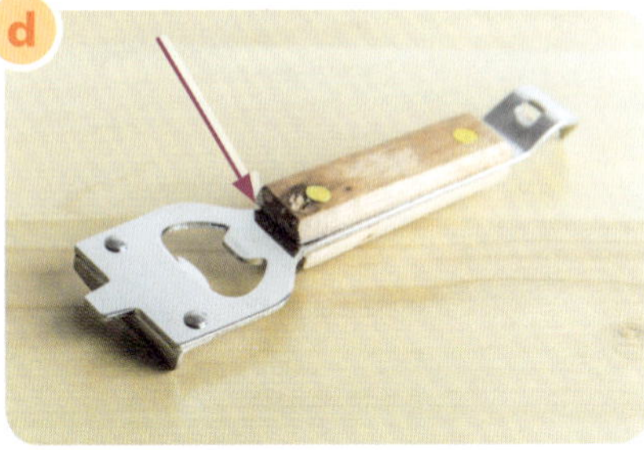

e

f

⑤ Do these complex machines need energy from people, electricity or fuel to work?

a

people

b

c

d

e

f

6 Label these simple tools and what we use them with. Match.

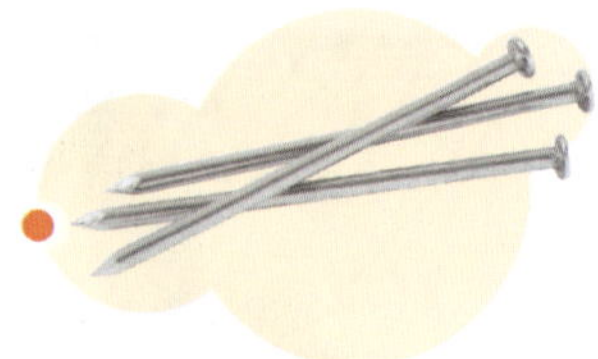

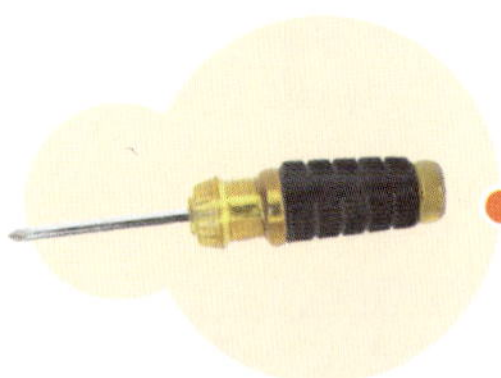

screwdriver

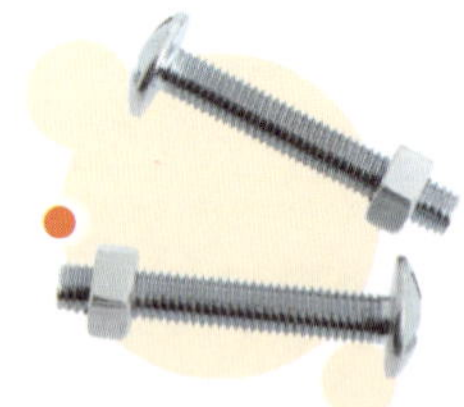

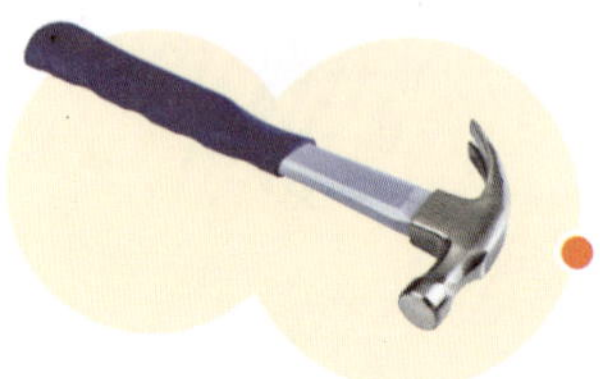

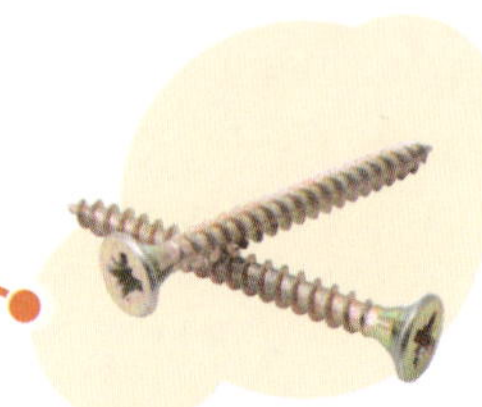

screws

7 Which tools do you use?

build a birdhouse

fix a bike

make a model

construct a bookshelf

a. *We use nails and a hammer to build a birdhouse.*

b.

c.

d.

8 Label the parts of the bike.

9 Read and complete the text about how a bike works using the words above.

A bike is a complex machine that's made up of many different parts. Each part has a special job to do. We hold the *handlebars* and use these to change direction. We push the ________ with our feet. When we push the pedals, the ________ moves round and this causes the ________ to spin. We use our hands to change the ________. When we pull the ____________, the brakes press against the wheels and the bike slows down or stops.

10 Identify the simple machines that make up a bike using the words in the box.

a. The chain and gears work as a ____________.

b. The handlebars work as a ____________.

c. The front and back wheels are ____________.

lever
wheels and axles
pulley

Find out at home!

1. Investigate simple machines at home or at school:

1. Read the information about simple machines.
2. Find simple machines in your home or at school.
3. Complete the table below.

Our homes and schools are full of complex machines which we use every day. These complex machines are made from simple machines. Here are some examples:

an inclined plane

a wedge

a lever

a wheel and axle

Name of machine	What simple machines does it have?

Skills check

1 Look and read. Write some words to complete the sentences below. You can use one, two or three words.

Wheelchairs

Some people need a wheelchair to move from one place to another. These complex machines make it possible for people to go to school or work, play with friends and participate in sports events.

Some wheelchairs are electronic and can move with the touch of a finger. Other simple machines, like inclined planes called ramps, help people in wheelchairs move up and down different levels.

We must remember to treat people in wheelchairs the same as everybody else – with respect and kindness.

a. People use wheelchairs to move from one place *to another*.

b. These ____________ machines make it possible for people to go to school or work.

c. Electronic wheelchairs can move with the touch ____________________.

d. A ramp is a simple machine that helps people move up and down different ____________.

e. We must remember to treat people in wheelchairs with ____________________.

Glosary

English	Your language	English	Your language

Unit 1: The human body

English	Your language	English	Your language
organ (n)		digest (v)	
function (n)		waste (n)	
torso (n)		pupil (n)	
limb (n)		iris (n)	
skeleton (n)		eyebrow (n)	
heart (n)		eyelid (n)	
brain (n)		earwax (n)	
blood (n)		eardrum (n)	
artery (n)		nostril (n)	
vein (n)		sour (adj)	
breathe (v)		sweet (adj)	
lung (n)		salty (adj)	
oxygen (n)		bitter (adj)	
carbon dioxide (n)		touch (v)	
		blind (adj)	

Unit 2: Look after yourself

English	Your language
balanced diet (n)	
healthy (adj)	
breakfast (n)	
lunch (n)	
dinner (n)	
carbohydrates (n)	
fibre (n)	
fruit and vegetables (n)	
dairy products (n)	
fats (n)	
proteins and iron (n)	
illness (n)	
calcium (n)	
bones (n)	

English	Your language
muscle (n)	
overweight (adj)	
cold and flu (n)	
stomach upset (n)	
tiredness (n)	
respiratory problems (n)	
tooth decay (n)	
obesity (n)	
lonely (adj)	
confident (adj)	
proud (adj)	
worried (adj)	
annoyed (adj)	

Glossary

English	Your language	English	Your language

Unit 3: Living things

English	Your language	English	Your language
man-made (adj)		bush (n)	
fungi (n)		tree (n)	
algae (n)		wheat (n)	
decompose (v)		kernel (n)	
nutrition (n)		woody (adj)	
reproduction (n)		branch (n)	
interaction (n)		thorn (n)	
sunlight (n)		trunk (n)	
seed (n)		deciduous (adj)	
spore (n)		evergreen (adj)	
alone (adj)		oak tree (n)	
root (n)		pine tree (n)	
climb (v)		fossil (n)	
stem (n)		change (v)	
grass (n)		environment (n)	

English	Your language	English	Your language

Unit 4: Mammals and birds

English	Your language	English	Your language
compost (n)	____________	lamb (n)	____________
feather (n)	____________	piglet (n)	____________
leather (n)	____________	chick (n)	____________
farm (n)	____________	incubate (v)	____________
field (n)	____________	litter (n)	____________
hay (n)	____________	develop (v)	____________
grain (n)	____________	fur (n)	____________
shed (n)	____________	flippers (n)	____________
feed (n)	____________	waterproof (adj)	____________
coop (n)	____________	beak (n)	____________
corn (n)	____________	nest (n)	____________
calf (n)	____________		

Glossary

English	Your language	English	Your language

Unit 5: Reptiles, amphibians and fish

English	Your language	English	Your language
hatch (v)		lose (v)	
scales (n)		gills (n)	
slither (v)		shoal (n)	
damp (adj)		pack (n)	
newt (n)		school (of fish) (n)	
moist (adj)		fin (n)	
hide (v)		ray (n)	
frighten (v)		seahorse (n)	
predator (n)		eel (n)	
webbed (adj)		camouflage (n)	
tadpole (n)			

Unit 6: Invertebrates

English	Your language	English	Your language
classify (v)		earthworm (n)	
exoskeleton (n)		starfish (n)	
thorax (n)		mantis (n)	
abdomen (n)		dragonfly (n)	
antennae (n)		ant (n)	
claw (n)		grasshopper (n)	
tentacles (n)		mandible (n)	
wasp (n)		hard wing case (n)	
spider (n)		life cycle (n)	
centipede (n)		larvae (n)	
crab (n)		caterpillar (n)	
snail (n)		attach (v)	
mussel (n)		chrysalis (n)	
squid (n)		emerge (v)	
jellyfish (n)			

Glossary

English	Your language	English	Your language

Unit 7: Matter, materials and mixtures

English	Your language	English	Your language
rigid (adj)		stretch (v)	
rough (adj)		rubber band (n)	
resistant (adj)		burn (v)	
smooth (adj)		combustion (n)	
fragile (adj)		ash (n)	
flexible (adj)		oxidation (n)	
absorbent (adj)		rust (n)	
property (n)		mixture (n)	
shape (n)		filter (v)	
size (n)		sieve (v)	
state (n)		evaporate (v)	
liquid (n)		cotton (n)	
solid (n)		slate (n)	
bend (v)		iron (n)	
twist (v)		crude oil (n)	
press (v)			

English	Your language
Unit 8: Energy	
light (n)	
movement (n)	
heat (n)	
electricity (n)	
sound (n)	
kinetic energy (n)	
chemical energy (n)	
thermal energy (n)	
sound energy (n)	
electrical energy (n)	

English	Your language
light energy (n)	
light bulb (n)	
engine (n)	
drill (n)	
coal (n)	
mine (v)	
solar energy (n)	
wind farm (n)	
wind turbine (n)	
hydroelectric power station (n)	

Glossary

English	Your language	English	Your language

Unit 9: Machines

English	Your language
simple machine (n)	
complex machine (n)	
inclined plane (n)	
pulley (n)	
screw (n)	
wedge (n)	
wheel and axis (n)	
lever (n)	
hammer (n)	
screwdriver (n)	
nuts and bolts (n)	
spanner (n)	
saw (n)	
cart (n)	
crane (n)	